T0008968

EDITED BY HELEN EXLEY

Published in 2019 by Helen Exley®LONDON in Great Britain.
Illustration by Juliette Clarke © Helen Exley Creative Ltd 2019.
All the words by Amanda Bell, Dalton Exley, Pamela Dugdale, Charlotte Gray,
Hannah C. Klein, Stuart & Linda Macfarlane, Pam Brown, Linda Gibson and
Odile Dormeuil © Helen Exley Creative Ltd 2019.
Design, selection and arrangement © Helen Exley Creative Ltd 2019.
The moral right of the author has been asserted.

ISBN: 978-1-78485-184-2

12 11 10 9 8 7 6 5 4 3 2 1

OTHER BOOKS IN THE SERIES

Be You!   *Be Confident!*   *Be Brave!*
Be a Rebel!   *Be Positive!*

OTHER BOOKS BY HELEN EXLEY

365 Happy Days!   The little book of Smiles   Yes to life! 365

The Secrets of Happiness 365   The book of Positive Thoughts

Helen Exley®LONDON
16 Chalk Hill, Watford, Herts WD19 4BG, UK
www.helenexley.com

Be Happy!

Helen Exley

Don't worry
about a thing.
For every little thing
gonna be all right.

BOB MARLEY 1945 – 1981

I ncrease your happy times,
letting yourself go;
follow your desire and best advantage.
And "do your thing"
while you are still on this earth,
According to the command
of your heart.

AFRICAN PROVERB

When I went to school,
they asked me what I wanted to be
when I grew up.
I wrote down "happy".
They told me I didn't understand
the assignment and I told them
they didn't understand life.

JOHN LENNON 1940 – 1980

Have fun! Enjoy the years
that lie ahead.
Open your arms to all delight
– of flowers and music, every lovely
thing. Of bold adventure and
astonishment. Of love.
Of friends you've yet to meet.
Be brave. Be curious. Be courteous.
Discover a wider world.

PAM BROWN

Be HAPPY Be Free

MARTIN BURNETT, AGE 10

Dance as though
no one is watching.
Love as though
you've never been hurt.
Sing as though
no one can hear you.
Live as though
heaven is on earth.

AUTHOR UNKNOWN

Most of us miss out on life's big prizes.
The Pulitzer, the Nobel, Oscars, Emmys,
Grammys. But we are all eligible for life's
smallest pleasures. A pat on the back.
A kiss behind the ear. A four-pound
barramundi. A full moon. An empty parking
space. A crackling fire. A great meal.
A glorious sunset. Hot soup. Cold beer.
A laugh with your mates.
Don't fret about getting life's grand awards.
Enjoy its tiny delights.
There are plenty there for all of us.

AUTHOR UNKNOWN

Enjoy the little things
of life. There may
come a time
when you realise they
were the big things.

ROBERT BRAULT

I wish you dreams of quiet meadows
deep in flowers and grass,
of oceans calm
and flecked with silver,
of islands hushed by gentle waves,
of countries of your own invention,
of easy talk with friends,
of roads leading to a reunion,
of sorrow comforted,
of hope restored.

PAM BROWN

All people have a sweetness
in their life.
That is what helps them to go on.
It is towards that they turn
when they feel too worn out.

ALBERT CAMUS 1913 – 1960

Listen to the music
you love.
Surround yourself
with things that make you
feel spoiled.
Love life!
Be happy!

PAMELA DUGDALE

Life is fun
Life is happiness
Life is gladness
Life is loving
Life is helping
Life is gentleness
Life is laughter
Oh life is beautiful.

ALLISON HUDDART, AGE 10

You can have anything you want
if you want it desperately enough.
You must want it with an exuberance
that erupts through the skin
and joins the energy
that created the world.

SHEILA GRAHAM

May the road
rise to meet you.
May the wind
be always at your back,
the sunshine warm
upon your face,
the rain fall soft
upon your fields…

IRISH BLESSING

Grow your own laughter.
Catch your own dreams.
Fashion each day
of your future into a life
filled with excitement,
joy and contentment.

AMANDA BELL

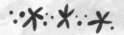

Sing every day.
Dance every day.
Skip every day.
Smile every day.
Have fun.

STUART & LINDA MACFARLANE

No more brooding,

No more despondency.

Your life will become

The beauty of a rose,

The song of the dawn,

The dance of twilight.

SRI CHINMOY 1931 – 2007

I wish you
love.
I wish you
friendship.
I wish you
a job worth doing.
I wish you
the gifts of courage and perception.
I wish you
the happiest of lives.

CHARLOTTE GRAY

Be happy for this moment

Enjoy each day, cherish each moment.
Each is a rainbow
that will light your path through life.

LINDA GIBSON

I hope you find joy
in the great things of life –
but also in the little things.
A flower, a song,
a butterfly on your hand.

ELLEN LEVINE

his moment is your life.

OMAR KHAYYAM 1048 – 1131

Travel to see the flowers in Spring!

Walk the wild moor!

Go and find the beautiful places.

I hope you'll make time

to see the world.

CHARLOTTE GRAY

Be gentle with yourself.
Do not criticise or reprimand.
You are good and you are kind.
You have a right to be happy.

BRIAN CLYDE

I think of life itself now as a wonderful play
that I've written for myself...
and so my purpose is to have the utmost fun
playing my part.

SHIRLEY MACLAINE, B. 1934

Laugh a lot,
love a lot,
live forever.

BRIAN CLYDE

Take time to be friendly –

It is the road to happiness.

Take time to dream –

It is hitching your wagon to a star.

Take time to love and to be loved –

It is the privilege of the gods.

Take time to look around –

It is too short a day to be selfish.

Take time to laugh –

It is the music of the soul.

FROM AN OLD ENGLISH SAMPLER

Find kind, gentle friends.
Find fun friends to share free,
happy days.
Enjoy being with them.
May there always be
friends to share your laughter,
your troubles
and your victories.

HANNAH C. KLEIN

May you find the work,
the friends, the opportunities
and the love you long for.
Meet the future with hope
and courage, enthusiasm,
energy and joy.
Take them all and from
them build a life that's
worth the living.

PAMELA DUGDALE

"Just living is not enough",
said the butterfly.
"One must have sunshine,
freedom,
and a little flower."

HANS CHRISTIAN ANDERSEN 1805 – 1875

Splash in puddles,
Laugh with the wind,
Be happy!
Make happiness
your purpose in life.

STUART & LINDA MACFARLANE

Don't evaluate your life in terms
of achievements, trivial or monumental,
along the way… Instead, wake up
and appreciate everything you encounter
along the path. Enjoy the flowers
that are there for your pleasure.
Tune in to the sunrise, the little children,
the laughter, the rain, and the birds.
Drink it all in… there is no way to happiness;
happiness is the way.

DR. WAYNE W. DYER, B. 1940

There are only two ways
to live your life.
One is as though nothing
is a miracle.
The other is as though
everything is a miracle.

ALBERT EINSTEIN 1879 – 1955

I wish you laughter.
Spluttering laughter,
whooping laughter,
the helpless silent laughter
that sends you to the floor in tears.
Giggling laughter, heads together.
The shared laughter in the
dark of an auditorium.
The laughter that crowns success,
that springs from joy.
Kind laughter,
laughter that reaches out and
gathers others to itself.
And never mind who stares.

CHARLOTTE GRAY

*When you finally
allow yourself to trust joy
and embrace it,
you will find
you dance with everything.*

EMMANUEL

Be happy.
Happiness
lives all about you
– only waiting
to be recognised.
Find it.
Delight in it.
Share it.

PAM BROWN

Keep on looking for
the bright, bright skies;
Keep on hoping
that the sun will rise;
Keep on singing
when the whole world sighs,
And you'll get there
in the morning.

HENRY HARRY THACKER BURLEIGH
1866 – 1949

Don't waste a minute
not being happy.
If one window closes,
run to the next window,
or break down a door.

BROOKE SHIELDS

A smile starts on the lips.
A grin spreads to the eyes.
A chuckle comes from the belly;
but a good laugh
bursts forth from the soul,
Overflows,
and bubbles all around.

CAROLYN BIRMINGHAM

Yesterday's gone. Tomorrow's invented.
We only ever have today, this moment.
This life. Don't waste it.
At least stop to enjoy it.
So brief a spell we have,
and if happiness,
like some magic dust,
touches us, even briefly,
then smile and treasure it.

DALTON EXLEY

Keep
a green tree
in our heart
and perhaps
a singing bird
will come.

CHINESE PROVERB

Let go the sad times,
hold on to the glad times,
the picnics and parties and fun,
the tingle and glow of a walk
in the snow, the lazy days
sprawled in the sun.

PAMELA DUGDALE

Close your eyes. You might
try saying… something like this:
"The sun is shining overhead.
The sky is blue and sparkling.
Nature is calm and in control
of the world – and I,
as nature's child, am in tune
with the Universe."

DALE CARNEGIE 1888 – 1955

I wish you days
of quiet contentment
and days of joy.
Days of discovery.
Days of achievement.
And even on dull days
a little flash of sunlight.

PAM BROWN

With freedom,
books, flowers
and the moon,
who could not be
happy?

OSCAR WILDE 1854 – 1900

And remember this:
every time we laugh, we take a kink
out of the chain of life.

JOSH BILLINGS 1818 – 1885

Dance first

Happy dreams!
Happy wakenings!
Happy days!

PAMELA DUGDALE

Think later.

SAMUEL BECKETT 1906 – 1989

Life -
the most wonderful
fairground attraction
of all -
enjoy the ride.

AMANDA BELL

The real thing in life, is to be happy.
The older I get the more convinced I am
that no ambition is worth pursuing except
that of being rather happier…
I would not give a brass button to be
the greatest general that ever won a battle
or even think the greatest statesman that
ever bamboozled the world.
But I should like to be quite happy
to the last day of my life, and to be able
to inspire affection at the age of eighty…

WILFRED SCAWEN BLUNT 1840 – 1922

It is a morning in early Spring and the sun
is rising, reflecting its pale shafts upon the wall.
The first delicate sprays of the plum blossom
lean from a jar on the table.
Everywhere is very quiet, like a holy day.
A blackbird, a missel thrush and a robin
are singing. Mists lie over the fields
and the sky is tender blue.
At rest in bed in the bare little room,
pervaded by light and peace and the sweet
airs of morning, there is happiness.

CLARE CAMERON 1896 – 1983

Slow down and enjoy life.
It's not only the scenery
you miss by going too fast –
you also miss
the sense of where you're going
and why.

EDDIE CANTOR 1892 – 1964

There is beauty around us,
in things large and small,
in friends, family, the countryside,
a singing bird. Stop to reflect,
to give thanks,
to contemplate the gift of another day.
Touch the wonders of life
and rejoice.

ANTON CHEKHOV 1860 – 1904

Everything is a gift of the universe –
even joy, anger, jealously,
frustration, or separateness.
Everything is perfect either for our growth
or our enjoyment.

KEN KEYES JR. 1921 – 1995

May you find happiness in a quiet,
perpetual rejoicing in small events.

HANNAH C. KLEIN

I wish you joy
in the great things of life –
but also in the little things.
A flower, a bird,
the friendship of a cat.

PAM BROWN

If you get the choice
of sitting it out
and looking at life,
or dancing
your way through it,
I hope you dance!

FR BRIAN D'ARCY, B. 1945

To a young heart everything is fun.

CHARLES DICKENS 1812 – 1870

Remember the story of the old man
who on his deathbed said he'd had
a lot of trouble in his life,
most of which had never happened.
Don't make too much
of this thing they call life.
It's all too brief a moment
in time.
Just be.
Just be happy.

DALTON EXLEY

The best thing is when you enjoy…

– mornings of glad anticipation

– the happiness of friendship

– adventures with happy endings

– exactly the amount of adventure

that you need

– promises kept, discoveries made,

goals planned and reached…

HANNAH C. KLEIN

Sixty seconds
in every minute,
3,600 in every hour,
each one a precious
diamond to cherish
and enjoy.

STUART & LINDA MACFARLANE

The world is inhabited
by a species whose
whole reason for being
is the pursuit of happiness.
Do your bit for mankind.
BE HAPPY.

BRIAN CLYDE

At the end of the day, life is about
being happy, being who you are,
and I feel like we are so blessed
to have the support system
and the best family to really
just support each other no matter what
we're going through.

KIM KARDASHIAN, B. 1980

Do not put off
till tomorrow
what can be enjoyed
today.

JOSH BILLINGS 1818 – 1885

Be content with what you have;
rejoice in the way things are.
When you realise
there is nothing lacking,
the whole world belongs to you.

LAO TZU 604 B.C. – 531 B.C.

There is not one day of your life
that is worth wasting being sad.
Be Happy!

STUART & LINDA MACFARLANE

If you are wise

I like it most when you're full of hope –
when you believe you're the bees' knees.
Always believe it. You're the greatest!

CHARLOTTE GRAY

I have come to realise making yourself happy is most important. Never be ashamed of how you feel. You have the right to feel any emotion you want, and do what makes you happy. That's my life motto.

DEMI LOVATO

laugh. MARTIAL c.40 – c.104

T o see a World
in a Grain of Sand,
And a Heaven
in a Wild Flower,
Hold infinity
in the palm of your hand
and Eternity
in an hour.

WILLIAM BLAKE 1757 – 1827

Happiness does not come
boxed and labelled.
Cannot be supplied
by manufacturers.
Grows wild.
Is all about you.
Free.

HANNAH C. KLEIN

Throw
your
heart
out in
front
of you
And
run ahead
to catch it.

ARAB PROVERB

We should never be so busy
that we miss out on the sheer wonder
of being alive.

EMILY DICKINSON 1830 – 1886

Wake up with a smile
make this the best day
of your life.

STUART & LINDA MACFARLANE

Never,
never,
never
give up.
And remember
to dance
a little.

GLORIA STEINEM, B. 1934

Look past your thoughts
so you drink
the pure nectar
of this moment.

JALAL AL-DIN MUHAMMAD RUMI
1207 – 1273

Listen to the passion of your soul,
set the wings of your spirit free;
and let not a single song go unsung.

SYLVANA ROSSETTI

To fill the hour –
that is happiness;
to fill the hour,
and leave no crevice for a repentance
or an approval.

RALPH WALDO EMERSON 1803 – 1882

My advice is: Go outside, to the fields,
enjoy nature and the sunshine,
go out and try to recapture happiness...

ANNE FRANK 1929 – 1945

*Life is a journey,
and if you fall in love
with the journey,
you will be in love
forever.*

PETER HAGERTY

I wish you
the joy of discovery.
Of learning,
of ideas,
and stretching your thoughts.

CHARLOTTE GRAY

I wish you quiet, perpetual rejoicing
in all small things.

ODILE DORMEUIL

Happiness is intrinsic,
it's an internal thing.
When you build it into yourself,
no external circumstances
can take it away.

LEO BUSCAGLIA 1924 – 1998

This is the best day
the world has ever seen.
Tomorrow will be better.

R. A. CAMPBELL

Look at everything
as though you were seeing it
either for the first
or last time.
Then your time
will be filled with glory.

BETTY SMITH

You're only
fully alive when
you're happy.
Go For It!

LINDA GIBSON

To see the fire that warms you,
or better yet, to cut the wood that feeds
the fire that warms you; to see the spring
where the water bubbles up that slakes
your thirst, and to dip your pail into it;
to see the beams that are the stay
of your four walls, and the timbers
that uphold the roof that shelters you;
to be in direct and personal contact
with the sources of your material life;
to want no extras, no shields;

to find the universal elements enough;
to find the air and the water exhilarating;
to be refreshed by a morning walk
or an evening saunter; to find a quest
of wild berries more satisfying than a gift
of tropical fruit; to be thrilled by the stars
at night; to be elated over a bird's nest,
or over a wild flower in spring
– these are some of the rewards
of the simple life.

JOHN BURROUGHS 1837 – 1921

Some days
there won't be a song
in your heart.
Sing anyway.

EMORY AUSTIN

A little health,
a little wealth,
a little house
and freedom!

FROM AN OLD ENGLISH SAMPLER

I wish you nights
pin-pricked with stars,
sheets newly ironed,
arms welcoming and quiet sleep.

PAMELA DUGDALE

Let happiness surprise you,
like a seashell
hidden in the sand…
a treasure…
waiting to be discovered.

SUSAN SQUELLATI FLORENCE

Learn the sweet magic
of a cheerful face;
Not always smiling, but at least serene.

OLIVER WENDELL HOLMES SNR. 1809 – 1894

Deep peace, pure white of the moon to you;

Deep peace, pure green of the grass to you;

Deep peace, pure brown of the earth to you;

Deep peace, pure grey of the dew to you,

Deep peace, pure blue of the sky to you!

Deep peace of the running wave to you,

Deep peace of the flowing air to you,

Deep peace of the quiet earth to you.

FIONA MACLEOD 1855 – 1905

When
one
flower
blooms,
it is
spring
everywhere.

ZEN MONK

I wish you small pleasures –
home-baked bread, fresh eggs,
sun after rain, a smile in passing.
And I wish you tremendous pleasures –
love and music, discovery and art.

PAMELA DUGDALE

Doing what you like is freedom.
Liking what you do is happiness.

FRANK TYGER

*You've got everything
you need to be happy,
a wonderful world and
the ability to love.*

AMANDA BELL

Happiness and contentment
will always be the two things
I wish for you.

SIÂN E. MORGAN, B. 1973

Happiness seeps in
like a beautiful light,
the light of a beautiful summer evening
settling on all around.

DALTON EXLEY

Red... blue... yellow... green...
purple... violet... pink...
fill your heart with colour.

LINDA GIBSON

You are surrounded by gifts
every living moment of every day.
Let yourself feel appreciation for their
presence in your life and take the time
to acknowledge their splendor.

LON G. NUNGESSER

May the coming years
bring you new hopes,
new beginnings,
new adventures,
new discoveries.

CHARLOTTE GRAY

The weather forecast says
"Rain! Rain! Rain!"
but your heart says
"Sun! Sun! Sun!"

STUART & LINDA MACFARLANE

The best day i

today! AUTHOR UNKNOWN

May the wind be gentle
May the waves be calm
May the elements smile on all our wishes.

WOLFGANG AMADEUS MOZART 1756 – 1791